Start Your Own
JEWELRY
BUSINESS

YOUR STEP-BY-STEP GUIDE TO SUCCESS

PETRU VANTU

INTRODUCTION

So, you might have heard that fashion jewelry is the most lucrative business in the world. Or, you might have a passion for shiny baubles and gifts. Or, you might be looking for a low risk, low capital business that you can invest in. Whether you are the next jewelry name brand or moonlighting on eBay after work, this ebook will help you to make sure you are informed about this business.

The number one thing you have to know about the jewelry trade is that it is not easy. If you think by making a purchase of some company's minimum order and sell it here and there and somehow turn it into a million dollar business, then you are setting up for disappointment. I am not trying to scare you off, but I want to explain the pitfalls and help you succeed. Fashion jewelry is a great business. And, there is money to be made. You can succeed with the right strategy, commitment, and execution. Make sure you take advantage of all the resources the Fashion Jewelry Industry has available to you.

Here's a complete guide on how you can start/ build your very own Jewellery Business to an enviable height

Thanks again for downloading this book, I'm sure you'll enjoy reading it!

Content

INTRODUCTION

• Copyright 2017 By (PETER FREEMAN) All Right Reserved.

Content

CHAPTER ONE

INTRODUCTION TO JEWELRY BUSINESS

    History of Jewelry

    Are You Ready to Go Into Business?

    Starting Your Own Jewelry Business -What You Must Consider

    First Steps To Starting Your Own Jewellery Business

    Finding Your Niche When Starting a Jewelry Busniess

    Business Model and It's Importance in Jewelry Business

    The Key Elements of a Business Model

    Starting Your Jewelry Business with Wholesale

    How to Start a Jewelry Business Using Wholesale Trade Shows

    Wholesale Pre-Packs

    When to Buy Jewelry When Starting a Jewelry Business

    Organizing A Jewelry Business Store

    What a Jewelry Designer Does

Astounding Types of Metal Jewelry

Quick Tips For Working With A Jewelry Design Company

Using Popular Colors In Jewelry Business

Creative Packaging in Jewelry Business

CHAPTER TWO

ONLINE JEWELRY BUSINESS

Why Has The Online Jewelry Business Blossomed?

Categories of An Online Jewelry Store

10 Tips To Create A Successful Online Jewelry Business

Unique Ways To Promote Your Jewelry Business

Essential Information to Include on Jewelry Business Cards:

Websites For Jewelry Businesses

Creating an Inexpensive Jewelry Website

Using Blogs to Make Sales for Jewelry Business

Making Training Videos To Promote Jewelry Business

Social Media Strategies for Jewelry Business

Advantages of Using Social Media Optimization For Jewelry Business

Top Social Media Tools of Online Jewelry Marketing

Other Smaller And Effective Social Media Strategy For Jewelry Online Marketing

How to Find Small Social Networks

Jewelry Software And Starting Your Own Business

Selling Your Jewelry on Amazon

Amazon Features

Your Products Get Spotted

A-to-z Guarantee Program

CHAPTER THREE

GARNISHING YOUR JEWELRY STORE

Simple Ways to Brighten Up Your Jewelry Store

Install CCTV Cameras In Your Jewelry Stores

How to Consolidate Your Jewelry Business's Reputation

CONCLUSION

CHAPTER ONE

INTRODUCTION TO JEWELRY BUSINESS

History of Jewelry

Jewelery is something that humans have enjoyed throughout almost the entirety of their history, regardless of the religion, race, or culture. Jewelry in one form or another has been ⬜uite popular throughout many of the cultures of history, as a form of expression, and also as a form of showing your social status within a given culture. However, the jewelry has taken many different shapes and forms over that period of time.

The materials used to manufacture the jewelry have changed ⬜uite a bit since the early days of jewelry. Early jewelry consisted of necklaces made of natural elements, or beads that had been shaped. Later, after we were able to harvest precious metals, we began to find jewelry that utilized gold and other metals, as a way to convey well.

Depending on the culture, jewelry may function as either a fashion or a sign of artistic expression. In some cultures, jewelry is used to attract mates, with a wide variety of different kinds of jewelry available. Precious metals and gemstones have been used throughout the history of jewelry, in bowl Greek and Roman cultures, as well as early Egyptian culture, and in order to convey a message. Often times, early Greek and Roman jewelry, would be highly affected by trade with neighboring cultures, and varied in style, depending on what type of resources were available to them. This was the earliest beginnings of jewelry wholesalers in the world, with jewelry traders traveling large distances, in order to effectively trade and sell jewelry.

Jewelry during the middle-age was affected heavily by Christianity, as it spread around the world. During that time, many of the different types of jewelry symbolized events from the Bible, or pieces of the Christian faith. At this time, Christian organizations became responsible for manufacturing and distributing a large amount of the world's jewelry while spreading the religion.

Jewelry during the Renaissance period was very different from other periods. Prior to this, jewelry had mostly been used to symbolize something you believed in, or to show off your wealth. However, during the Renaissance.

Jewelry became used for body decoration, in an effort to improve the presentation of the individual, which had differed from its use in many previous cultures.

Today, jewelry is viewed as many different things. Although it is also used to increase the beauty of an individual, it is also utilized for artistic expression, with costume jewelry wholesale being very popular among individuals that are looking to make a point with their jewelry, while fashion jewelry wholesale businesses have thrived, as jewelry has ingrained itself in the lives of individuals that are interested in fashion. It is clear that jewelry, and wearing ornaments, is something that is deeply ingrained throughout human history. In almost every major culture, jewelry has played some role. Whether that role is to display the wealth of the individual, to make a point to or convey a message, or simply to increase the beauty of the individual, jewelry has been a part of every major culture throughout human history in one form or another, and does not appear to be going anywhere anytime soon.

Are You Ready to Go Into Business?

The biggest fear that people have about going into business is loss of income. Consider the fact that if you do not show up for work on a regular job there is loss of income. And if your boss decides to sell or close the business you are out of an income.

Being self-employed is guaranteed success because you are confident in your personal work ethics and you trust and know that you have the will and the discipline to show up for work every day to earn your desired income.

Being self-employed allows you to earn as much money as you would like to have as you set the limits.

Recall what caused you to think about self-employment. Something or many things on the following list motivated you to take a look at being your own boss.

- Do you like your job?
- Do you like your boss?
- Do you like your paycheck?
- Do you like your work schedule?
- Do you like commuting to and from work?
- Do you like meetings?
- Do you like the dress code?
- Do you like transportation costs?
- Do you like the limited opportunities?
- Do you like the office politics?
- Do you like the pressures and stress load of the job?
- Do you like the working environment?

- Are you prepared to go into business?

These Are The Qualities of Readiness:

- You are motivated.
- You are ambitious and have the energy to support your goals.
- You are disciplined.
- You finish what you start.

Are You Ready To Learn How To Start A Jewelry Business?

- You are blessed with creativity.
- You love making jewelry.
- You have both skill and experience making jewelry.
- You have an open mind to learn.
- You just need direction on how to get started and earning money as soon as possible.

Everyone has dreams. Whether you really want to take that first step towards realizing them is no one's decision but yours. And that first step can be the hardest... for good reason. Because realizing your dreams has nothing to do with talent, finances, whether your jewelry is good enough, your level of experience and education or what your husband, wife or friends have to say about it. It has everything to do with giving yourself permission to step forward.

Opening up your own business starts with believing in yourself. No one else will ever benefit from your talent if you don't put it out there. Not only do following your dreams help your well-being, your family and your faith in yourself, think of all the people you can help beautify with the sparkling and uni☐ue creations that you inspire.

Starting a jewelry business has nothing to do with how much money you have to invest like most people would think. That's just an excuse. Of course, that's the main reason people give. You can start out slowly with resources that literally cost next to nothing.

If you already make jewelry for a hobby or for friends and family, you have already spent a good part of the investment needed: tools, gems, materials, workspace, and findings.

Other things that are needed to bring a business to life can be found on the cheap: business license, logos, branding ideas, a website, brochures, and packaging.

Starting Your Own Jewelry Business -

What You Must Consider

Many people set up their own jewelry business after making jewelry for family members and close friends. Since everyone around them thinks that they should begin a jewelry business, they are getting even greater enjoyment out of it. On the other hand, there are those who want to buy jewelry from distributors and sell at their own premises. All these are good reasons to start a jewelry business, but you need to learn how you can start the business and see it grow. It is true that a number of jewelry businesses start and fail to succeed beyond the first year. On the other hand, there are those that grow to see extensions or branches while others succeed in selling the products online on sites like eBay.

Just the sound of that phrase conjures up pictures in the mind of the entrepreneur. Freedom. Money. Fulfillment. Starting your own jewelry business is an opportunity available to millions of people in the great world in which we live, but with every opportunity, there come liabilities. As wise business people, we are compelled to consider the advantages of a start-up business.To begin, let's look at the benefits.

1. Freedom. Is there anything more valuable than freedom? Since the presence of freedom allows for all the other benefits we find in life, it stands to reason freedom would have to be at the top of the list of pros for starting your own business. If you can pick your own trade or service, do it in the manner in which you choose (with few limitations), do it for as long as you choose, and then sell that business to someone else when you choose... you have freedom, and freedom is not only the platform from which all other business benefits spring from, it is the greatest single benefit.

Freedom to make your own choices, work when you want to, vacation when you want to... what price freedom?

2. Money. More money has been made and can be made by self-directed enterprise than any other way of work. If you need proof of this, look to history. Read stories of entrepreneurs. You can go back hundreds of years, or you can look to your parent's generation. Either way, you will find the fortunes of this country have been built on the foundation of small business.

There are massive fortunes in big business, to be sure, but every big business began as a small business; one or several individuals identifying needs and wants and seeking out ways to fill those needs and wants in a profitable manner. You may be able to secure a decent salary at a good company, but the money you can make in private enterprise dwarfs it many times over.

3. Fulfillment. Fulfillment is harder to define than the other more tangible aspects of business enterprise. While running a business can bring huge financial rewards, deeper and more meaningful are the personal development gains that come from it. Whether or not one makes a lot of money, if he or she can experience personal development and growth as a result of their business venture, they have profited. Some entrepreneurs find ways to build a lifestyle business, based upon what they love most and are talented at doing. Others find the very process of building a company of any kind brings out qualities in themselves they were not even aware of.

Starting your own jewelry business is a journey of personal fulfillment. There is more satisfaction in creating your own enterprise than in developing someone else's, because your business is of you, and about you, and for you.

First Steps To Starting Your Own Jewellery Business

Before putting up that sign and opening for Jewelry business, there is a significant amount of work you will need to do. The following paragraphs include some of the things you will need to complete before you can open your business.

• Assess The Need

Is there really a need for the goods or services you are going to offer? Many new business owners overlook this very important point. People will often go into business offering a product or service they are good at producing but never really considered if the product or service would be useful to other people. The easiest way to find out is to ask people what they want or need.

• Research The Competition

Now that you have determined that there is indeed a need for what you are offering, it is time to find out who else offers the same goods or services. Find out who your serious competitors are. You want to know what makes people want to do business with them. You also need to know what it is about your competitor that people don't like.

Be sure to not imitate the competitor's faults. Also, you will need to determine if your market will support another business like the one you are opening. Do not assume that you will "steal" your competition's customers. People are creatures of habit and it may be difficult for them to change to an unknown business.

- Will You Make A Profit

This one is a tricky one because there are so many variables that affect the profitability of a business. But, you have to analyze everything you know (and don't know) about the business you are starting. Everyone says it great to owns a Jewellery business doing something you "love", but how long do you think you will be doing that thing you love if you don't make money? You are at a point in your venture where you need to create a "Break Even Analysis".

A break-even analysis is just a document where you list your projected expenses for a 12 month period to determine the dollar amount your business needs to generate just to pay the bills. You then need to look at your projected sales for the same period of time and try to make a determination if this is worth it. The first 2 or 3 years you will probably show a loss, but after that 5th year, you should see decent profits if the business is viable. If you can't show a profit after year 4 on paper, it is probably not a good idea to start that business. You will need to be honest about sales and expenses, avoid the temptation of being overly optimistic.

- Seek Professional Help

Now is not the time to start cutting corners. A good accountant, lawyer, and any other business or financial professional are worth their weight in gold. If you don't currently have these people as a part of your business team, you need to find them fast. Ask friends and relatives if they have any recommendations and be sure to check references. Don't hire a family law attorney when you need a corporate lawyer just because it is your 3rd cousin. Good professionals (notice the emphasis on good) can save you thousands of dollars over the life of your business by helping you to avoid pitfalls and obstacles. An attorney should review every scrap of paper before you sign your name.

- Location, Location, Location

You will need to find a few locations they may work for your business. Before you sign that lease, ask yourself if your type of business needs to be in a "high profile" area to succeed or can you do just as well off the main strip.

This is important because the high profile areas usually mean high rent. But if your businesses will depend on high profile, then high rent is going to be a cost of doing successful business. You may want to consider purchasing over renting, be sure you factor this into your startup costs as it may cost you a considerable amount more to buy, but it may save you thousands in the future. Be sure to have a lawyer review any lease or contract in advance.

- Your Gonna Need Money, Lots of Money

Be sure you determine your capital needs before open your business. In their optimism about owning a business, new business owners tend to underestimate the amount of money they will need to open and operate their business. This is probably one of the biggest mistakes new business owners make. In my opinion, you should determine your financial needs by listing your startup costs, then list your monthly operational costs. Now pretend that your first customer will not make a purchase until your 3rd month of business. If I were you, I would be sure to have enough capital to operate my business without 1 cent in sales for at least 3 months, you never know what will happen.

• Now You Need A Good Plan

Once you have completed the previous steps, you are ready to complete the most important step, your business plan. A good business plan is like a map, it helps you find the path you need to take to get you to your destination. Also, if you plan to seek financing for your business, most banks and investors will require a business plans. Even if you don't plan to borrow money, you should create a business plan. And you should make it a point to review the business plan frequently. This practice helps keep you on track and will help get your business to the next level.

Finding Your Niche When Starting a Jewelry Busniess

A niche is a refined topic stemming from a larger topic. It further concentrates products and ideas down to specific target to where customers can identify their needs or concerns. This is a bunch of geek-speak to mean that consumers are always looking for specifics when they buy: is it something for their children, is it environmentally friendly, is it handmade or one of a kind? Of course, not all consumers are looking for a niche...some don't mind purchasing at one-stop-shops or one-size-fits-all. But if someone was to search for a specific gemstone or style, either online or at a mall, would your jewelry be accessible?

Advertising the uniqueness of your jewelry is key in attracting those consumers that want/need something different. Some niches are created for those who have a favorite gem such as Amber. Almost everyone has a favorite color or gem that they would purchase over another. Some niches are created from conscience consumers such as the conflict-free diamonds. And some niches are simply specifics such as men's jewelry or wedding jewelry...pieces that they would only purchase at a particular time. Look at your line closely...how can you find a niche embedded in general beauty of your pieces?

Describing your jewelry with a niche in mind helps set you apart in a number of ways. In online marketing, it is important to use niche keywords to help search engines find you better. If you specialize in a certain gemstone, customers will seek you out as the "go to" person and drive across town to buy from you. Being a specialist in a niche will create loyalty and exclusivity with your customers.

Before you start anything, I'll advise you to find a few profitable jewelry niches. You can use Google Search Engine to do the research. Please remember this is very important steps to take. Please do not target competitive niches like Heart Jewelry, Animal Jewelry, Engagement Ring, Eternity Ring and etc.

Google Search Engine show that 60,500,000 result for just 'Silver Jewelry'. We don't say that you should not target 'Silver Jewelry'. They are just competitive and very challenging if you go into it. Pay Per Click Advertising will easily cost you more.

Try to target the sub-niches of 'Silver Jewelry'.

Let me give you an example:

Heart Jewelry - Triple Heart / 3 Heart Silver Ring, 2 Floating Heart Necklace, Pave Heart Pendant and etc.

Animal Jewelry - Running Horse Silver Pendant, Baby CZ Gold Elephant Ring and etc.

Engagement Ring - 3mm CZ Silver Eternity Ring, 2 Stone Red CZ Wedding Ring, 10 mm Oval Engagement Ring.

Do you get the idea? Above are just a few examples of the sub-niches of the big jewelry niche. Please do take note that jewelry is a broad area that consists of Silver, Gold or Platinum.

Business Model and It's Importance in Jewelry Business

The concept and type of business models have constantly evolved throughout the years and have had a long history that dates back to several years.

When it comes to establishing a new Jewelry business it is important that you are well aware of the various business model types. Your entrepreneurship is sure not to run successfully if you have a wrong one model. There are certain templates that already exist and all you need to do is to use one of them to your benefit. You cannot change or modify the business patterns and this is the most interesting aspect of it. The success of your venture would depend on choosing the most appropriate model or you can even combine 2 or 3 business model types to be used in your endeavor. What is the Most Popular Out of them especially when it comes to Jewelry Business ventures?

Off-Line and On-Line Business Models

- **Offline**: Jewelry wholesalers and retailers often start up on a low scale. Both usually begin by opening a shop in a preferred location. It is a good idea to invest in good equipment, a proper location and gradually scale up. One may also choose to become franchisees of reputable labels to cash in on the brand value of the products. It definitely helps if one has a proper understanding of the commodities market since the prices of gold, silver, and other precious metals are influenced by various factors that are reflected in the commodity market.
- **Online**: The model is catching on these days, in which manufacturers, designers, retailers, and wholesalers have either developed an e-commerce portal or linked up with major online shopping networks to showcase their products. The benefit of the online model is that it is not constrained by geographical boundaries and is the easiest way to go international. The Internet jewelry business is growing exponentially thanks to technology, superior supply chain models and rapid penetration of the web.
- **The Hybrid Model:** The hybrid model involves manufacturers and wholesalers using a combination of both the offline and the online models. In today's commercial environment it is foolish to ignore the power of the Internet, and establishedmanufacturers and wholesalers often choose to sell through conventional trading channels as well as the Internet. This way they are able to maximize their reach and capture as much market as possible.

It is important to note that since the consumer is extremely fickle, one must be prepared to face the possibility of a design becoming outdated in a very short time. One must, therefore, be innovative and offer diverse designs that can be mixed and matched with other styles. It is crucial to continue learning about the cultures of other countries and try to incorporate as much as one can to create patterns that are unique and appealing to a variety of customers.

The Key Elements of a Business Model

Simply put a business model not only should give you a key analysis on the projection of your business but also should give you a clear understanding on how to survive and compete within your market.

Let's take a look at simple and effective ways that a business model can be improved.

1. Customer Value Proposition: This translates to providing a solid method for providing a service or beneficial product. A customer value proposition has to be more than a simple service, like free voice over Internet Protocol communications or dedicated database organization. These are great services to offer, but that's the point: that is all that those models offer. There is a strong temptation for companies to mention as many benefits as they possibly can. The downside is that this clouds the point of the business and confuses investors as to what the purpose is.

2. Establish A Foothold: No matter how well-done your customer value proposition is, it is worthless unless you can get some actual customers! This is an expensive process, even more so if your target customers are already mainstreamed. A popular and profitable approach is to locate a customer niche of early adopters. Early adopters usually are the first to try new things and this makes them invaluable for spreading the word about your business. In addition, these niche customers can provide feedback to help perfect your model. Niche adopters can also create a lot of hype about your product or service, which is great because it is basically free, effective marketing.

3.   Distinguish   Yourself: Innovative entrepreneurs are the ones that survived the crash and prospered. What can your business do to distinguish itself from competitors in the same industry or customer niche?

• **Effective Pricing Methods:** The best way to undercut the competition is to try new pricing methods. You can even disrupt an entire industry by changing the way your business prices its products and services.

Starting Your Jewelry Business with

Wholesale

Obviously, the way to start, as with any business, is with wholesale. This will enable you to make your profits. By shopping wholesale, you are getting incredible prices and a huge amount of stock; which you will turn around and sell for more than what you got it for.

This is especially good with wholesale jewelry as it can become very pricey not to buy this way. It only makes sense to shop wholesale when starting your business. Whether it is for wholesale fashion jewelry or just plain wholesale jewelry, it is worth your while. Once your business is up and running, you will start to see all of your hard earned invested money, start to reach its potential; especially when you are shopping wholesale.

To get started on wholesale shopping, make sure you have your license that all wholesale businesses recognize. Every state has its own rules so just make sure you are getting the license applicable to you. Almost all wholesale businesses will then recognize you, so you should feel free to then shop around at your leisure; always looking around for the best-discounted prices and the places that are best for you.

Once everything is set in motion, like your location and the types of jewelry you will be selling, shop for your wholesale jewelry and wholesale fashion jewelry. You will be able to start your business pronto once you have finished that. You are sure to see your business booming if you advertise correctly.

You can not go wrong when shopping wholesale jewelry; you are getting affordable prices in order to start your business. Then, you will be able to have affordable, attractive prices. Just make sure you are hitting the right crowds; women, or their significant others.

How to Start a Jewelry Business Using Wholesale Trade Shows

Trade shows are a great way to expose your jewelry line to a ton of retail store owners shopping to fill their establishments. Some trade shows are regional in nature and some attract buyers from all over the world.

If you are ready to take your wholesale accounts to the next level, trade shows are the best place to be. The set up is quite a bit different than an art show but is easily learned. Basically, instead of stock, you will concentrate on displaying samples.

You'll need really great lighting to make your pieces sparkle and some interactive media to show your manufacturing techniques such as a TV monitor that plays a looped video.

You will also need everything to make multiple sales not only at the show but to supply buyers the needed materials to take home with them before making a decision. Bring plenty of order forms, catalogs, brochures, credit applications and promotional materials. The displays you use are not only for your samples but also to show what buyers can expect from you in terms of displays you can send them to their stores.

Trade shows are usually well attended and are a bustle of activity in a fast-paced environment. Buyers have thousands of booths to visit in just a couple of days, collecting catalogs and making decisions. The impression you make in terms of professionalism and expertise will go along way in keeping your brand fresh in their minds for as long as possible.

Wholesale Pre-Packs

Selling on a major scale to multiple accounts is a far different animal than selling at art shows or the mall. Attracting store buyers and getting them interested in your line is not difficult, but store owners do things a certain way based on how the trade has been doing it for years.

Sales reps and manufacturers offer what is called a pre-pack to save time and money. A pre-pack is a collection of a manufacturer's best sellers along with displays and signs, all for one price. You would think that most store owners would pick out the pieces they want to buy one by one, but that is not the case. Some buyers do of course pick their own pieces, but most realize that when it comes to jewelry and gemstones, they are not the expert... you are.

Sure, buyers know what they like when they see it, but what they like may not necessarily be what sells the hottest. You as the manufacturer of your own line knows that best. Compiling all of your hottest movers saves the buyer time in trying to figure that out. Also, a pre-pack can act like a "bulk" purchase in the buyer's mind. Let them know that the pre-pack saves them "X" amount of money over a bunch of single items.

Pre-packs should contain all of the displays necessary to set up the jewelry lines that are in the pack. All the store buyer has to do is open the box and set it up...done! This saves the buyer time as well. Price your pre-pack to a simple round number such as $250, $400 or $650. Make a couple of different packages and price points so the buyer has options to make a major purchase or one just to try your line out. Making it easy on the buyer will make them spend more money.

When to Buy Jewelry When Starting a Jewelry Business

Sometime after you open up a mall store or even something as small as a cart, you'll realize that it can look very empty compared to your craft show table. Making a jump to a larger selling space will challenge you with how to fill in the dead areas. No matter how beautiful your jewelry is, a customer will be turned off quickly seeing an empty cart and shop elsewhere. Keeping your store or cart full of exciting inventory can be difficult if you're not sure what to fill it with.

There are two thoughts of how to buy additional jewelry for your store without disrupting your brand image. You could find very complimentary pieces made by another manufacturer that you can put straight out onto your table. This could be a pretty costly option that could eat into your bottom line. Another option is to buy complimentary looking gemstones and findings and put them together yourself. This is a far cheaper alternative that provided me with tons of filler lines.

Don't feel that filler lines will cheapen your main artwork jewelry pieces. With carefully selecting gem colors and complimentary metals, they can fit right in nicely. This strategy will also expand your price points wider to accommodate younger buyers that may have only $20.00 or less to spend without having to lower the prices of your signature pieces. If you purchase outside lines remember to buy or assemble in sets to maximize the sales.

Even less expensive alternatives include putting consignment pieces in your store from other artists that you may know or purchase lines from a jewelry store going out of business. Filling out your store or cart will give you the freedom to attract a varied customer base, widen your price points, keep a solid inventory and make a full and visually exciting store. All these techniques will increase your profitability while keeping your sanity.

Organizing A Jewelry Business Store

The transition from hobbyist to professional jewelry designer will have you moving from the kitchen table to a workbench. The kitchen table served you well when test marketing your jewelry wear with friends, neighbors, relatives, and fellow workers. A number of orders is telling you to start making professional changes in order to be able to increase your production.

Here are indepth knowledge on how to go about organizing your new jewelry business office/showroom

      1. Office area:

• Placement of telephone, computer, order taking materials, and delivery schedules.

• File cabinet for legal forms, business invoices, order forms and receipts, accounting and tax

records, and photo catalog for jewelry designs.

• Computer for notification and saving all notices for jewelry shows and events in your community or out-of-state functions, online jewelry sales, and monitoring website, and online orders from customers or for business jewelry supplies, and other jewelry making accessories.

2. Workbench:

A comfortable working height.

• Ergonomically correct sitting stool or chair.

• Proper lighting.
• Self-standing or mounted magnifying glass.
• Sectional container for jewelry tools.
• Bead, beading thread, wire sectional, and fastener containers for work in progress necessities.
• Proper measuring equipment and jewelry boards.

- Notepads.

    3. Inventory storage:

- Pegboard for hanging strings of beads.

- Plastic containers for storing loose beads.

- Thread peg holder for storing spools of wire, threading, etc.

- Containers holding finished work for quality control review.

- Containers to store jewelry by individual colors and sizes.

- Library shelving for professional instructional videos, jewelry books, trade magazines, and personal designs and ideas.

    4. Display setup

Display holders' for necklaces, bracelets, and rings.

- Various theme accessories such as weddings and other personal celebrations, national holidays, and seasonal sales.
- Attractively draped table to enhance jewelry setups.
- Mirrors for customers.
- Mini glass or acrylic display cases.
- Large glass display cases.
- Business sign and business card holder.
- Sign up sheet.

Regardless of whether you have customers occasionally coming to view the jewelry display or not, this area needs to be set up for photo shoots of your merchandise.

What a Jewelry Designer Does

A jewelry designer seems like such a cool thing to do. They have quite a history as jewelry has always been popular regardless of the century. Jewellery designers were originally called goldsmiths even in Ancient Greece. Many designers are simply carrying on family tradition and in many countries, this is certainly the case. They grew up around gold and silver and precious gems and learned how to make jewelry from their family, often from a young age.

A modern day example of this is the Paloma Picasso, daughter of the famous painter, who designs jewelry for Tiffany. Her pieces have a dynamic look and most certainly she has learned a lot about design from her father.

There are jewelry designers who work for individuals. You can work with a designer to have your Jewelry Business supplies, for example. There will be an initial consultation where you get to know the designer and he or she gets to understand you a little better. You can explain what you would like and the designer will sketch some preliminary designs (or even use a computer design program) to see what you think. You can go from there until you both agree on the perfect designs.

The designer also has to know exactly how the work involved is done. Otherwise, he could design things that are impossible to make. This is why designers usually make the jewelry as well as just design them. That means they have to have knowledge of many things, including mounting which is the actual frame for the piece involved and this often means forming as well as drilling so that the gem will fit exactly. The final piece will need to be polished. Sometimes other processes are involved such as electro-plating which means layering a precious metal like gold onto a base metal. Sometimes jewelry is engraved or metal is welded together - today this can be done by laser. Enamel jewelry is also an intricate process.

It is only through knowing your choice and preferences and doing all the work involved that the jewelry designer can work on his or her own designs. Even today, goldsmiths in many countries mean going to a special school as well as becoming an apprentice and this process can take around three years.

Astounding Types of Metal Jewelry

Huge collections of jewelry can turn your starting process frustrating and confusing. Therefore, it's wise to know about the basic types of metal jewelry before starting your entrepreneur process. If you are quite aware of the models, then starting a jewelry business process would be comfortable and worthy. Here are some of the popular metal jewelry that are dominating the present world:

•Gold jewelry:

Gold jewelry has its own beauty due to the attractive nature of the gold. It is one of the precious jewelry that is still retaining its topmost position among the different metal jewelry. There are different types of gold jewelry that varies depending upon a number of alloys add to it. Purest gold is said to be 24 karats, but it is extremely soft. So, other alloys are added to make it stronger and long-lasting. During gold jewelry shopping, you must be ☐uite aware of its karat rate which determines the worth of the jewelry. Depending upon a number of metals mixed with gold, you can find different standards of gold jewelry such as pure gold, gold filled and gold plated. Therefore, it's important to carefully buy gold, because gold-plated jewels have very little percentage of gold, but looks like a pure gold.

•Platinum jewelry:

This metal is considered more precious because it is available in less ⬜uantity. This jewelry is expensive than the gold jewelry. Platinum will scratch more easily than gold and it provides anti⬜ue look for the user.

•Silver jewelry:

Silver is also a soft metal, so it is mixed with other alloys to make them stronger. It is not used often as gold. It is less expensive than gold, but make not have much glow or attractiveness.

•Steel jewelry:

Presently, steel jewelry is emerging as a modern jewelry especially among young people due to its uni☐ue design and trendy look. Steel jewelry is available for all ages under different categories such as kids' jewelry, unisex jewelry, man jewelry and woman jewelry. One of the important reasons for its increasing demand is its medical uses. Steel has high resistance to corrosion and hypo-allergenic properties, which makes it into a medical instrument. Most of the body jewelry is made up of steel due to its healing power. Now, you can also find several trendy kids jewelry in steel. Besides, steel jewelry has many more merits such as beautiful metal, less expensive, long-lasting, and its modern style.

Quick Tips For Working With A Jewelry Design Company

Working with a jewelry design company to create the perfect piece for prospective customers can be a rewarding experience. Taking these eight tips into consideration can make the experience as smooth as a polished gemstone.

When you work with a custom jewelry design company, you can get a ring, pendant, broach or other piece of personalized jewelry that's absolutely unlike anything anyone has ever worn before. All the details are up to you -- and to the tastes and sensibilities of your designer. But you have an obligation to make sure you're clear about what you want and when you want it if you want your piece to come out right.

Here are quick tips for dealing with a jewelry design company that are intended to make like easier for your customers:

1. Give the designer drawings, photos or models if you have them. Don't think you'll offend the designer if you show him or her your ideas from the beginning. Providing a visual reference for the artist will save misunderstandings and make sure you get the piece you desire.

2. Keep an open mind. Your designer will almost certainly be faced with design decisions that aren't covered in your discussions, notes or drawings. Leave those small details to the discretion of the artists. No one can see inside your head, but your finished product should be fairly similar to what you envisioned.

3. When ordering a ring, don't leave sizing to chance and measurements. Let your designer be aware of the exact measurement to make sure he or she has the sizing absolutely perfect. You're paying for custom work, so you should make sure it fits perfectly.

4. Give a reasonable deadline with some padding. Things happen in custom design, so allow for some deviation to your delivery schedule. But also, add some padding. If you must have the piece for a certain customer, allow some extra time in case of delays. Get a delivery date in writing, if necessary.

5. Ask about the off-season if there's no rush. Valentine's Day, summer wedding season and the holidays are busy for craftspeople of all sorts, so avoid ordering during these times if there's no rush for your piece. Be sure to find out when your chosen designer isn't busy.

6. Get cost ranges in writing. You should know how much your customers ring, pendant or other custom-designed jewelry piece is going to cost them. Get prices in writing so there are no surprises. If you want changes that aren't the result of errors, expect to pay extra. Ask □uestions and understand what's included in your price. Know the refund policy too.

7. If you supply stones or raw materials, determine who's responsible for loss, damage or recutting errors. You want to work with a jeweler who's insured, but not every designer is willing to take responsibility for problems that may be inherent in the materials you provide.

When you and your custom jewelry design company understand each other, things are certain to go smoothly. When you don't, there will likely be hard feelings and an array of unpleasantness that could have been avoided.

Using Popular Colors In Jewelry Business

When making jewelry no matter what the style, you need to be aware of the popular colors of each season and how they affect jewelry sales. Colors

change often according to which season it is: Spring, Summer, etc... And they clothing manufacturers keep a close eye out on what is the going color trends. Certain colors reflect the seasons directly such as Yellow or Gold going into Spring and earth tones such as browns and greens heading into Fall.

What you have to be aware of as jewelry artists are which colors clothing designers will be making for particular season and making sure that your gemstones and jewelry designs will match properly. Getting the trend information ahead of the game and far enough in advance to pick the corresponding colored gemstones is critical to making sales. If the consumer can find very little on your table to match the popular colors of their current wardrobe, you may find your sales lacking.

No matter what kind of jewelry making techniques you have, whether it be silversmithing, hammered gold, wire wrapping or beading, you'll need to pay attention to the popular seasonal colors and ac□uire the proper gemstones, beads, and glass. This includes wooden beads, lampworking, precious metals or any of the techni□ues you work with. If you purchase jewelry from wholesale accounts, pay special attention to color. Wholesalers will try and dump last seasons colors for cheap to get rid of excess stock, but you don't want any part of this no matter how cheap it is. You will be stuck with jewelry no one will buy.

If you are selling your jewelry wholesale to store owners, be aware that they are some of the first to educate themselves on the current color trends. Buying jewelry for their stores without doing the proper trends research can cost them dearly. If your pieces are not part of the season color trends, they will purchase elsewhere. Take time to be on top of the color trends as they present themselves. It will make you successful in the end.

C

reative Packaging in Jewelry Business

It's amazing how many jewelry makers neglect their packaging when running their jewelry businesses. Age old marketing dictates that jewelry packaging has always been a bit fancier than regular consumer items. Why is this? Because most jewelry is bought to give as gifts for special occasions. So people have to come to expect that the packaging should reflect the occasion. It doesn't have to do much with the expense as some would think.

A television can easily cost much more than a piece of expensive jewelry but is rarely given as a gift or saved for occasions.

If you have ever seen a woman's eyes light up when seeing an intimately and beautifully wrapped gift box before she even opens it, it is something to behold. That speaks volumes about the treasure inside, so it is very important that each piece you sell is enveloped in beauty. Packaging doesn't have to be expensive, just creative. It needs to reflect the talent of the artist, the beauty of the gem, the special occasion at hand and the prestige of the uniqueness.

Packaging can range from fancy hand-carved wooden boxes to gift bags with colorful tissue paper and everything in between. I've seen packaging that was fancier than the jewelry piece...so be it! Your wrappings will speak volumes about your business and can even make your jewelry look better. On the cheap end, you can get small gift bags and bundles of tissue paper from a dollar store or order in bulk from packing wholesalers. There is an endless list of jewelry box manufacturers on the Internet.

Remember that the packaging should hold your jewelry in place until she opens it. There are boxes for all kinds of pieces that keep the piece secure: ring pads, bracelet boxes, necklace pads and earring cards that hold the pieces in place so it's not a jumbled mess when the package is opened. Whatever packaging you use is up to you, but make sure it compliments the talent and beauty of your pieces.

CHAPTER TWO

ONLINE JEWELRY BUSINESS

Why Has The Online Jewelry Business Blossomed?

The advent of the internet has spelled a happy period both for jewelry businesses as well as shoppers. Most top jewelry brands and jewelry designers today, apart from having their own physical shops are trading and selling online. Small-scale businesses and traders not to be left behind too have jumped the bandwagon and that's why you see a cluster of online stores today. That's not all, in the next 5 years, it is estimated that the online imitation jewelry business itself would grow 3 to 4 fold. So therein comes the question, why has the online jewelry business taking precedence over the age-old system of physical shops?

While there is no arguing that buying online lacks the personal touch (since you can't touch and feel the product), there are several counter benefits of the medium. The first advantage being you can literally buy from anywhere across the globe provided you have internet access. So for example, someone in the US who wishes to buy this intricately carved designer jewelry from India can do just so by making the payment online and the product would be delivered to his/her home. So you don't physically need to go to the shop to buying anything.

Secondly, online shops are open 24 hours 7 days a week, so it is like a portable store where you can pop in at any time. Thirdly the range of items that you can browse through at a given point of time in an online store is gigantic. In a physical shop, you won't have this luxury but in the online world, you can search, choose and make concrete shopping decisions. Plus you don't have to undergo the trouble of visiting the shop because everything is delivered to you at your doorstep.

Shopping online too has also become much safer compared to previous years as companies today care a lot about their online identity and hence strive to provide a much better shopping experience. Secondly with so many shops jostling for online space, retaining customers has become a priority. So the risks involved with buying jewelry online has reduced considerably.

With most of us being connected to the internet either through personal computers, laptops, mobiles, etc, it is no wonder then that the numbers are only expected to grow in coming years. It is a win-win situation for both consumers and business and the future indeed looks bright for the online jewelry industry.

Categories of An Online Jewelry Store

The online jewelry store has been created just because there is a site selling a product and you as the consumer has the power to be able to get that item by means of using your laptop or PC. The item is then mailed out to you. An online store might not be just in use by means of a website, it may, in addition, have a high street store as well.

    I. The first form of an online jewelry store is the one that has its doors open to the public domain via the high street. It is the customary store where you are able to physically walk into it and admire the items of jewelry that are up for sale. In the past, these shops may possibly never have had a website, although, to date, this is very improbable. The net has become such a magnificent means of marketing, practically all high street stores have internet websites as well. In recent times, they have also transformed their establishments into "online businesses", as a result of offering clients the facility to be able to make their acⅢuisitions using a web page.

II. The next style of an online jewelry store is the kind of store that is totally internet based. This means that there is no shop, similar to your traditional store where you would walk in and inspect the pieces up for sale. This form of an online store is a sensational modern notion. It usually means that you as the consumer are able to make purchases at bargain prices. These types of stores don't have the high overhead costs like customary shops. They do not have to pay employees to work for them also they don't have to shell out rent on a storefront. These two things in a small establishment can be detrimental to making a small business a flourishing one.

III. The last kind of online jewelry store is an auction website. There are websites such as eBay where you are able to pay for items by way of an auction system. If you prefer to use a means like auction, to buy a piece of jewelry, you will have to be ready to of course not be the winning bidder. This can be □uite disappointing if you are wanting to buy that "special" item. On the provison you are not shopping for something, in particular, auction websites can be a terrific alternative way to go.

10 Tips To Create A Successful Online Jewelry Business

Here we offer you 10 valuable tips to help you give your online jewelry business a unique twist over the competition:

1. Show Pride In What You Do

Show and talk about your jewelry business with pride. Do not see it as a side activity you are doing just to earn more money, but find your connection to it and discover why you were attracted to it in the first place. If you are proud of what you sell, others will be proud of buying it.

2. Build Relationships

A jewelry business is a great opportunity to meet interesting people and connect with them; you never know who you may meet. Focus on creating strong relationships with your clients by adding extra value to your pieces; the Internet is a superb way to do that.

3. Respond Emails Promptly

If possible, reply to emails within the same day. Whether the writer is a potential customer or just a visitor, answer with care because you never know when someone may become a client.

4. Prepare To Answer Questions

You will receive all kinds of ⬜uestions and re⬜uests, so be ready to talk about materials and related issues, the creation process, stone origin, your jewelry wholesaler, shipping and payment options, how you see the pieces you sell, and their true value.

5. Be Knowledgeable, But Don't Lecture

Your clients will want to confirm how much you know about your business but they are probably not looking for a lesson. Ask for opinions instead, because you can get a lot of ideas from them.

6. Always Tell The Truth And Honor Your Business

If you have a great product, you don't need to trick people into buying it. Tell them the truth about what best suits them and give them information so that they can make a good decision.

7. Have Patience

Do not take people's comments personally. If they think your prices are high, it is because they don't know everything that goes into the creation and selling of a piece; this is why it is important that you make them look worth their money by adding some other kind of value, perhaps, nice packaging, a set of cleaning instructions or history booklet, or an authenticity certificate.

8. Gift Your Customers

Include a thank you gift with every purchase; it can be something small and nice like a cell phone charm, or a discount coupon for the next purchase.

9. A Promise Is A Commitment

Your jewelry is your responsibility until it reaches the buyer's hands. Make sure you have a safe shipping method and be accurate about delivery times and rates; the same goes for your return policy.

10. Stay Calm

There are many things that you can't control, thus, recognize this and do the best you can. Your clients have to feel you are in control even though you aren't because if you remain calm they know everything will be fine and they will be rewarded in one way or another. If you lose your composure, they will label you as unprofessional.

Unique Ways To Promote Your Jewelry Business

1. Mailing Lists

Customers have to see your products to be interested in buying them, so a mailing list is the best way to ensure they receive notification of new products, great sales, and seasonal promotions. In addition, having a mailing list is helpful because you can track your client base and reconnect with those who haven't placed an order in a while.

2. Home Parties Are a Great Way to Sell Your Work

Home parties have been used successfully to sell everything from cookware to naughty nighties; most of these small businesses are part of a large, organized national franchise, but the home party concept is also a perfect way for local crafters to market their wares.

If you'd like to try home parties, you need a plan. First, take a look at your inventory of jewelry; do you have enough pieces, in a large enough variety, to hold a party? Think about having coordinating pieces - necklace or pendant, earrings, rings, and bracelets, in five or six different designs. Have enough pieces of each so that you can sell the items individually or in sets.

Once you've decided what you want to sell and how many items you to need to have for sale, set a timeline for yourself, based on how long it will take you to craft the items, and then schedule your first party. If you have a friend, family member, or co-worker willing to host a party for you, that's great. Otherwise, put up flyers, along with copies of your business card, and send a press release to your local paper.

Fill your hostess in on how you plan to run the party, and make sure she lets her guests know that you plan to have the items for sale at the party. You may want to discuss her responsibilities; most home parties have light refreshments, and she'll need enough seating for all her guests, plus a clear tabletop for you to use as a display area.

During the party, make sure your jewelry is displayed attractively, and have inexpensive but attractive door prizes so that guests have an opportunity to win a small handcrafted item. It might be enough for you to display your work but think about working up a presentation for each collection, and show it around to guests.

Another good idea is to display a portfolio of high uality, color photos of more complex, expensive gifts for special ordering. And don't forget to collect the names of guests who are interested in hosting a jewelry party of their own!

You'll want to reward your hostess for having the party, so be sure you have a thank-you gift. You may want to allow the hostess to choose her favorite piece from your jewelry collection, or you may design a graduated gift selection, with the hostess gift based on the amount of money you make at the party.

If you know other crafters, consider offering to sell their craft items at the party for a commission. You may even want to create a small home party cooperative with several crafters, so you can each sell your own crafts and collect a commission on everyone else's work.

3. Holiday Gift Baskets

Women aren't your only clientele. Husbands, boyfriends, bosses, etc. are another huge market you can reach. By creating bundle deals or gift baskets for the holidays, you are preparing a fun and uni□ue gift that every woman would love. Include this information in your mailers so your clients can tell they're significant other what they want for the special day.

4. Before-and-Afters

The best way to sell your products is to show potential customers what they can do, to create an archive of before-and-after pictures showing your best Jewellery. These can be compiled in a binder which you can take with you to classes and appointments, but you can also use it in your marketing. If you really want to be bold, put your own before-and-after on your car signs! Customers will respond very well when they see how proud you are of your products.

1. **Gift boxes for your jewelry are the next important item to consider.** If your jewelry wholesaler doesn't supply these, you will have to source them at a packaging or gift-wrap wholesaler. Be sure to consider all the sizes you need for the different pieces you sell. If the boxes don't come with an inner liner you will have to put that in as well.

2. **Business Cards**

Business cards are the number one sign product for any business. Your business card shows your authority, reputation, and trustworthiness. By offering your card to a potential client or exchanging cards with another business professional, you're extending an offer to establish a business relationship. In addition, cards list your important contact information, so if the recipient needs any of your products, they have your card and know how to get in touch with you.

Essential Information to Include on Jewelry Business Cards:

Aside from printing your jewelry shop's name, address, and contact information, it is also important that you include what sort of jewelry you sell. People want to be presented with specifics. Your jewelry business cards would certainly ring a bell if specific information is printed on it.

Also, your jewelry business cards should have a professional and attractive look. The people you are selling your product would be those people who value appearances. If you have a dull-looking business card, people would have the impression that your jewelry are dull, too.

1.Car Signs

Most Jewelry businesses are run from one location, so to a certain extent, your car is your mobile office! Take advantage of this by covering your vehicle with car signs. Car magnets are a great choice because they can be removed if you don't want to advertise your business, or if you really want to make a bold statement, order a car window decal for your back window. These are highly-visible and give you lots of room to "sell" your Jewelleries. With car signs, wherever you go, your message goes with you!

2.Window Signs

If you have a storefront, use window signs to identify it. Vinyl decals and lettering are great for listing your business name, store hours, and contact information (phone number, website, etc.). An attractive storefront will get the attention of window shoppers and bring them inside to discover what you have to offer.

3.Yard Signs

Yard signs are versatile and portable, which means they can be placed in front of your home, outside your store or office, or even in the yard. There are materials for every budget, from economical corrugated plastic to long-lasting metal and aluminum.

4.Stickers

Stickers are a fun and unique way to promote your Jewellery business as they can be used almost anywhere. Print stickers of your company logo, or even of your best products, to distribute to customers. Consumers like to identify with their favorite brands, especially Jewelleries. It's not important where they use the sticker, but rather that they are distributed far and wide. Another great idea is to place a sticker with your name and contact information on all the products that you sell. If your customer lets a friend or family member borrow one of the Jewelry they bought from you, that person will see your information and might contact you!

Any of these products can be useful when building your Jewellery business. Look at your marketing budget (or set one if you haven't yet) to determine the most-effective product(s) for your money. Signs pay off quickly, and if you take care of them, they'll last a long time.

5.Poster

Use posters to advertise your Jewellery business to reach your market and get your desired sales outcome. Here are effective techni ues to maximize the advertising benefits from posters.

- **Instill curiosity.** Get your customer's attention first by infusing curiosity. Create poster ads that will leave them drawn and curious of your cosmetic business. Make well crafted, eye-catching and unique poster ads that can get their interest with just one look at your print material.
- **Give information.** Provide the basic information they need about your cosmetic business. Information about your contact number and address are necessary data needed to be included in your posters. Its product and services must be well presented. Put benefits they can get from you. Avoid exaggerated information that can turn off your customers from patronizing your cosmetic business.

- **Have an emotional appeal.** The decision for a purchase relies on an emotional and rational response of the consumers. Products and services that are trustworthy and credible give a good feeling to your cosmetic buyers. They are more attracted to cosmetic products which appeal to their emotions and gained their trusts.
- **Persuade to have an action.** Your poster ad should always create urgency for the consumers to choose your cosmetic business. Your print material should appear convincing and moving. It should encourage your customers to have that buying urge towards your cosmetic enterprise.

Websites For Jewelry Businesses

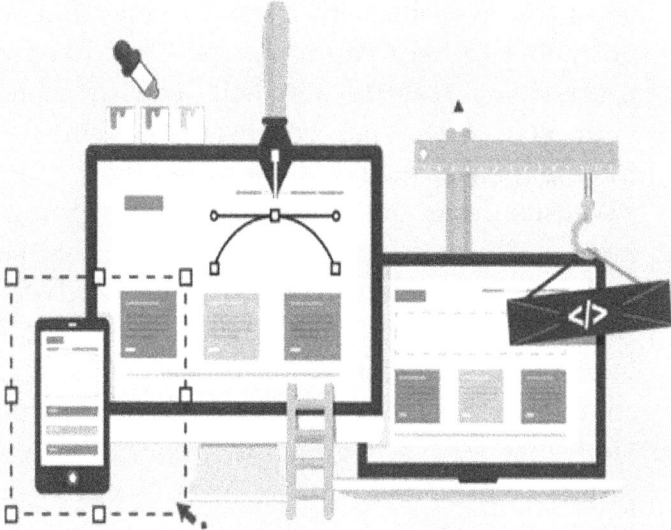

Do you have a website for your Jewellery business? If not, then you have omitted some very barely credible opportunities. How you can resolve this is by looking into web design so that you can have the website that is going to boost your earning possibilities. If you still not persuaded that website design is important for your business? Take a look at this:

•Some of the most profitable businesses have a website for there own. Actually, good-looking all of them do. It is important for them to increase their publicity to international markets as well as the domestic markets.

- Website designing is something that will provide your business a ꞏuality presence on the World Wide Web (internet). It is not sufficient to get a free website with a subdomain. That will not going to help you anymore. Only having a professional website will help you to achieve your goal that what you want to achieve in international as well as domestic market.
- Website designing means that you are going to have a direct interaction with your customers and your customers will buy your product or services through internet. Having a website for your business means that you are going to add completely new division on top of your business after that you are going to notice that your profits will boost up as you market your business.

Through this barely credible business that the World Wide Web (internet) has taken off the way your business was going on. If you were all building your own websites then, a most of us would be in trouble. Most of us do not have the time and most of us basically do not have all of the tools and knowledge to design and develop the website. That's what the web designing professional are for. They have all of the resources needed to design and develop a ꞏuality website for your business.

If your website not helpful in getting revenue for your business in spite of having a good design, content, layout, and graphics, the website is unable to produce income that you expect from your website. The answer to this problem most likely lies in the lack of usability in your site.

Creating an Inexpensive Jewelry Website

The new Wordpress.org software system is giving anyone who wants to have a presence on the web a chance to do so. This benefits jewelry makers greatly by giving them the freedom to create a place to do business cheaply and easily. Selling on Etsy and eBay is good, but creating your own portal is even better. Your website can also include educational information on gemstones, healing properties of minerals and cleaning tips among things.

WordPress software can upload to your hosting service in minutes with one click. It doesn't get any easier than this. You first need a hosting service such as HostGator.com to store the website on. This will cost you a whopping $9.99 a month. Then you buy a domain name, again only $9.00 a year or so. Then the rest is simple:

- Get your domain to point to your hosting. (HostGator will walk you through this)
- Upload your WordPress software with one-click "fantastico"
- Pick a theme (a theme is what your website will look like)
- Start adding pages to your WordPress site.
- Start adding products to your pages.
- Paste the shopping cart buttons under the products (PayPal, 1shoppingcart, Aweber, etc..)
- Start advertising! (Facebook, blogs, articles, Twitter, etc...)

Using Blogs to Make Sales for Jewelry Business

Blogging is a great way to advertise your jewelry business. Blogging takes advertising your line to a higher level than just putting pictures up of your jewelry with a "Buy now" button. You can use your blog posts to educate consumers, teach them how to clean their jewelry, provide show dates where you will be selling and even talk about celebrities and what they are wearing.

Creating a website provides an online platform from which to sell to or otherwise engage people. If your intent is simply to have a presence that people can visit online in order to contact you or view an about us page, think again. It's important to realize that you are doing 80% of the work (setting up the website) for only 20% of the value (by not taking advantage of easily adding content and attracting more people).

A Jewelry Website without fresh content is like starting a coffee shop in the basement with no advertising or signs. It's there, it may be a great service, but no one is ever going to find or use it. So what exactly does regular blogging achieve:

- **Increased Traction**- how often have you been to a website, got the information you needed, but stayed because you saw something else of interest? I'll wager fairly often.

- **Builds Trust**- people who visit a website regularly for information and content, by definition, have some level of trust in the content providers. This can translate into revenue down the line.
- **Showcase Knowledge & Expertise**- you don't have to give away trade secrets, but people benefiting from your blog can often decide that you are the go-to person if they ever need a Jewelry.
- **Increase Traffic From Search Engines -** Google and other search engines love new content. They'll visit your site more often if they know there is something new to index. You'll have more chance of appearing in search results the more you build up a reservoir of content.
- **Better Integration**- a blog can help to integrate you into the fabric of the Web, by allowing people to follow you via RSS, Twitter, and other mediums. This helps to boost your visibility via social means.
- **Enhanced SEO** - by increasing your readership it is possible to increase your Page Rank because people can start leaving comments (more content) and linking back to you.

The list goes on - but that should be enough to convince you to get going. Lots of people are hesitant or put off by the idea because they are worried that they don't know enough about writing web-enhanced, SEO focused content. Don't worry about. Write about topics related to your Jewelry business in a clear and concise way and the magic will happen all by itself.

Making Training Videos To Promote Jewelry Business

Video marketing on website social networks are all the rage towards advertising your business on the web. Publishing videos on YouTube, Facebook and a ton of other video hosting sites is as easy as pie and you can get thousands of views all that have a chance of leading those viewers to your jewelry website. And did I mention that video marketing was free? Yes. Opening up a YouTube account and video recording yourself costs nothing.

What kind of things can you shoot? The most interesting and powerful topics that people search for and want to see are instructional and educational in nature. They love to learn new techniques in jewelry creation and repair, information on healing minerals, design of displays and packaging and even cleaning and care tips. In other words, any topic that people want to know about jewelry you can teach them, build trust and credibility with that viewer and lead them to your website to purchase your line.

Videos are the perfect advertising medium of the Internet because it is so inexpensive to produce and there are hundreds of places to host your videos for free. You can share your video productions on Facebook and other social networks. Search engines love videos because it gives their customers a wide range of multimedia to choose from when they search for a topic. Show your expertise and build fans of your jewelry business the easy way. Turn yourself into a video star with video marketing. It's easier than you think if you have the proper training.

With all these ideas, it is essential to put in place good video asset management in order to protect and organize your videos for customer to enjoy. This can be done by asking associates how they manage their videos, or simply look for an experienced company that provides video asset management online.

Social Media Strategies for Jewelry Business

By now, you're sure to have heard about social media and how it's changing the way we communicate and interact with one another. From Facebook to YouTube and everything in-between, new social media websites sites are being launched on a regular basis, storming into our everyday lexicon.

All fine and well, but there's also much for Jewelry business to gain -understanding just how social media operate can be a huge advantage in terms of marketing your Jewelry business for free online, creating buzz, and obtaining customer feedback. According to SEO.com, "Social media marketing engages customers on a more personal level, and can rapidly create buzz around a product, brand, or business. It can also be more cost-effective than traditional forms of advertising and outreach".

Advantages of Using Social Media Optimization For Jewelry Business

Social Media Optimization is a mean of success for every business professionals as it provides a lot of advantages for online business. The popularity of SMO has increased over the last few years. In simple words, you can say that there is not any single business or company over the Internet who does not want to use this medium for better promotion of their website or products.

It is the authenticated medium for low-cost advertisement, where you can promote each and everything online and boost your client-base. With the help of social marketing, you can increase your web traffic as it provides the communication platform for your users. It also helps to gain attention from users more □uickly as compared to other media. As far as it affordability is concern, it is very affordable even for small businesses because you do not need high cost for the advertisement of your product.

•Improve Or Increase Your Network

It is the business saying that strength of the satisfied customer put you on a way of success. For this, you should have such type of media that allows a public networking which can influence your clients to buy your products.

Some community networking sites like Facebook and Twitter provide a user-friendly environment where every person can express himself or share their thoughts with others via emails, messages or even tweets. This can brings improvement and increment in your business network.

•Shorten The Gap

Social media provides a public platform on which you can develop personal relationships with different people that are very useful for your business. It provides a chance to know about the customer needs for some brand or product. You can answer their □ueries and satisfy them. So these media shorten the gap between business people and the public.

•Develop Your Online Reputation

It is very difficult to maintain a sustainable reputation because the internet is a very fast medium in which mouth of word travels faster than light. So you should be careful with it. SMO provides a clean, clear and well-reputed image if you will follow the rules and regulation.

- Low-Cost Advertising

Social media provides a most beneficial and interesting ways to advertise your products or services in a very low-cost. Once, you are connected with many of beneficial people then it is easier for you to share information about your products and services. You can also develop an interest among people by offering discounts or hampers to instant avail your services.

Top Social Media Tools of Online Jewelry Marketing

1. Facebook

This is a social media website that allows members to create personal as well as business profiles. It is an effective marketing tool because professionals can target their advertisements at specific regions, universities, and other customer bases. It also allows you to customize your personal and business profile so that it is unique and attractive. Facebook also provides a platform to promote discussions and comments on any topic that is pertinent to your business.

2. LinkedIn

LinkedIn allows its users to not only take advantage of all the benefits that any other social media site provides but, in addition, it provides graphs and various other analyses of connections between people. Since this website is mainly aimed at professionals, and there is not much personal information stored, people are usually more comfortable linking to a larger number of people using LinkedIn.

3. Twitter

Twitter is one of the best ways to connect with people. The limit of 140 characters per tweet helps to keep the tweets interestingly short and sweet. Everyone is on Twitter these days, and as a jewelry business owner, you have to go where your customer are. Signed up for a Twitter account with an appropriate handle so that your potential customers will know that you're boutique jewelry owner with uni ue items, and not just run of the mill products. Keep your tweets short, sweet and relevant in order to retain the interest of your followers. You're a celebrity and if you don't stay relevant to the customers.

Use the Twitter tools

There are many tools, widgets and advertising options available on Twitter, and you have to learn to make proper use of them with time and practice.

4. Plaxo:

This social media tool allows users to organize their business contacts, and make new contacts. It allows online business owners to not only connect with potential clients but also to find vendors and service providers that will help enhance their chances of success.

5. Flickr:

Although Flickr has been around for a while now, only recently are people realizing its potential as an online marketing tool. Using this website, members with online businesses in real estate, art, crafts and so on can post various photographs and promote discussions on them. They can also link to other people's Flickr pages, and by actively participating in comments sections and constantly updating photographs on Flickr, an online business owner can hope to effectively promote whatever product or service they have to offer.

Other Smaller And Effective Social Media Strategy For Jewelry Online Marketing

The best social media plans set forth measurable goals and work with any social venue.

We've discussed the guns like Facebook, Twitter, and LinkedIn. And other familiar names like Instagram, Pinterest, and Vine. However, these are just a drop in the bucket when it comes to all of the social media channels out there. And although they are "smaller," they still have tens or hundreds of thousands of users. If a large percentage of these users are in your target audience, you should be strongly considering adding it to your active social media strategy.

Here's the big benefit of smaller networks: barely any other business uses them!

Think about it. The biggest businesses need a huge audience, so they stick to the biggest social networks, they cannot survive on a couple dozen sales leads a day. But you can, and actually, you can thrive.

Small home Jewelry Business owners typically believe that they should just try to copy the big businesses...

This is the reason you see thousands of your competitors doing the exact same thing on Facebook and Instagram.

With smaller social channels, there is zero competition! You can ☐uickly amass followers and drive large amounts of traffic to your website in no time.

You start seeing faster responsiveness, better lead results, and more sales profit.

How to Find Small Social Networks

Expect to have to dig around for 30-60 minutes to find the best one for your business.

There are dozens of social networks that will work amazingly well for your niche audience, so you just need to spend the time finding the one that is right for your business.

Check out this list of social media channels you're probably not using and see if they have any potential for your Jewelry Business.

- Pheed

Pheed does more than letting users share video, text, music, and photos. It also offers live broadcasts and a pay-per-view option. Users set their own price for their content.

- Thumb

With Thumb, ask a question and get feedback from other users in real time. You can also share your own opinions and start conversations with peers on topics of interest.

- WhatsApp

WhatsApp is a cross-platform mobile messaging app. Users can send photos and videos, share their location, and create groups. There are thousands of Jewelry Business owners and other vendors with shippable merchandise that use WhatsApp on Instagram. It is a stress-free, confidential, and easy to use method for communicating with buyers around the country. By installing the app on your phone, you can text yours about their size, address, and other information without sharing it on social media.

- PicsArt

Is a photo editing app combined with a social network. Users can share their photos, discover images other users have uploaded, create a collage, co-edit, and enter contests.

- hi5

Is a social entertainment site. Users can use features similar to other social media sites like sharing photos, connecting with friends, and meeting new people. But hi5's big focus is on playable games.

- Buzznet

Members can share photos, journals, videos, and other content based on their interests. Most content centers around music and popular media. Content can be tagged and found on topic pages.

- About.me

Makes your personal homepage into a shareable digital business card. You can connect a resume, or "backstory," and add a mission statement to your profile. Users also gain access to stats on who visited their site, what they clicked on, and where they are from.

- Archetypes

Allows users create a customized "Story Page." Users take a ☐uiz to determine what their personal archetypes are and then that information is displayed on their page. Other features are included to highlight personal preferences and connect users with each other.

- Tsu

Gives its members a chance to share in earned revenue for the content they create. This method motivates users to create compelling content as well as gives them ownership in what they turn out. Membership is by invite only so it's a little exclusive.

How to Use these Smaller Sites:

Your goal is to find the few networks that are likely to have your target audience. All networks have their own purpose-their own niche(s).

For now, write down all the networks you think might have your target audience. As you work through navigating each site, you will ultimately determine if your choices are good networks to spend your time on.

Jewelry Software And Starting Your Own Business

A lot of people just imagine about opening their own business and never really do anything about it for the fear of failing. Jewelry software will be an advantage to you by making the means of starting your business not seem as off-putting.

Having a jewelry business you do not at the start need to give up your "full time - work for someone else" job until you are organized. Nevertheless, you will be able to also have your own business at the same time. Jewelry Software will make your beading life so much more convenient right from the very beginning.

If you are passionate about beading along with developing your own jewelry you will find that you more than likely already work a full-time job and do beading as a hobby. Why not test reversing this situation and bead full time and work as a hobby. This means you will be able to keep an "income stream" at the same time as your jewelry business gets off the ground. You then have more time to create what you love plus build up your compilation in order to market it. Jewelry software will guide you in order to help catalog your stock, as well as keep up with what you sell, how much you sell it for and at the same time you will be able to make a detailed file of all your customers.

The key thing you will need to do is set practical goals, and to make up a business plan. Preparing a business plan is very critical. If you are going to get a loan or a financier for the funding, you will want a formal business plan. The plan will need to be exact especially when it comes to the financial piece of your plan. While jewelry software may not supply you with a lot of information regarding this task, it is, however, an essential part of your business program.

While selecting your jewelry software make sure that it is able to produce the following:
- Track stock level along with manage inventory
- Automatic pricing
- Customer records
- Easy data export into excel format
- Instant professionally printed labels, invoices, and catalogs
- Notes and storage archive for designs details

- Easy backup and storage of data
- Invoice management and tracking
- Vendor tracking
- Tax calculations

Jewelry software programs will be able to make a considerable amount of your business more straightforward. In spite of this, there are still areas that you will want to pay attention to. You will be re□uired to check into a merchant account at different places such as PayPal for example. PayPal will let you take payments from clients purchasing over the internet as well as make payments to organizations when you purchase your stock. If you are going to transport any of your pieces, you will need to ensure you obtain low-cost jewelry packaging such as ring boxes. You should be able to get hold of such supply businesses from the internet effortlessly enough.

Create a website to give your consumers additional access to you and your products. Make use of Facebook along with Twitter and develop your jewelry business through social media. Working online and having your jewelry software should see your small business rise to new heights. In spite of this, don't fail to remember to persist with your face to face part of the business as this too is an essential facet of building an empire.

Ultimately jewelry software can help you with the side of the business that is commonly left to last or for someone else to take care of due to you being too occupied with the inspirational side of things. Jewelry software takes care of them, at times, more tedious side of your business.

Selling Your Jewelry on Amazon

Amazon is one of the most trusted online businesses. As leaders in the field on internet retailing, Amazon has the e-commerce technology and the traffic to sell your products to a global market.

Amazon Features

To give you a feel for the site, let us first take a look at the basic features offered by Amazon. Feel free to visit the site right now - do a search for any product and see what appears on your screen.

Features to notice:

Results always contain a professional photo or some sort of graphic of the product.

The price is made visible and it is combined with an offer, i.e. free shipping. Notice how the amount that is saved off of retail is made visible. This is an established advertising strategy - Amazon is telling people what the product is worth and that it´s presently selling for less than the amount that it is worth.

Amazon mentions the number of items that are in stock and the estimated time that the product will take to get to the customer. Shoppers are more inclined to buy an item when they are aware that the product's □uantity is limited. Time expectation is also a useful feature for most customers and sellers.

Amazon makes use of Cross-Selling and Up Selling. This refers a concept of selling that is based on product similarity or asking the customer if they would to purchase another product that compliments the first one that they bought i.e. when a customer considers one product; Amazon makes a mention of another product that might also interest the customer.

- **Reviews** - The 'Editorial Review´ section describes the product in great detail. Amazon also allows customers to review a product. These reviews are usually reliable, fair and act like testimonials about the product. All kinds of feedback can be useful for the seller.
- **Added Extras** - Amazon includes various other types of cross-selling and interactive devices i.e. customer discussions, a Listamania feature, Wiki Info etc. All these extras can be used to create interest around specific products or topics.

How It All Works:

Registration

For you to start selling your Jewelry on Amazon, the first thing you need to do is register. This is a simple process that re□uires you to fill out a short online form to register as an Individual seller. If you think that you will need to process more than 40 orders per month you should register as a Pro Merchant.

Upload Product Inventory

Amazon has made it really simple for you to upload your product inventory. After your registration, you have three options for submitting information that is related to your product:

•**Option 1:** Use the Add a Product feature on Seller Central to create one product at a time. If you are unfamiliar with Seller Central, all you need to know is that it is Web interface used to deal with all aspects of selling on Amazon.com. You can use this tool to add product information, make inventory updates and later on, handle orders as well as payments through it.

•**Option 2:** Make use of the Seller Desktop. This is a free and user-friendly desktop application that you can use to add products in bulk or individually to your inventory.

•**Option 3:** If you want to submit info about many products simultaneously, make use of the inventory files to create multiple products.

Your Products Get Spotted

By listing your Jewellery on Amazon, they reach millions of potential customers 24/7 - Amazon's traffic, now also becomes your traffic.

Your Jewelry gets Purchased

Buying a product from Amazon is not only convenient but also really simple and □uick. Your Jewelry is easily purchased at the click of a mouse.

Shipping

Essentially, you are in charge of shipping your product to its new owner. Amazon will notify you about the purchase via email when an order has been placed. All you have to do is, pack and ship your product to the customer. If you would prefer not to handle this section you could opt for the Fulfillment by Amazon option.

Money in Your Pocket

Amazon then does the payment to you via a direct deposit into your bank account. You will also be notified about this deposit via email as soon as your payment has been sent.

While we are on the subject of money, let me give you an outline of Fees involved in becoming a Seller on Amazon...

There are 2 major 'seller' packages that have been made available by Amazon.

If you are looking to sell only a few products or expect to have less than 40 orders placed per month, you would want to register as an Individual seller. The only fee involved here is a 'per product sold' fee of $0.99 - this means that you only pay $0.99 per product that you sell.

On the other hand, if you think that you will be selling much more than 40 products per month, you should sign up to be a Pro Merchant. Here should expect to pay a standard monthly subscription fee of $39.99 as well as a minor referral and closing fee when your products sell. These fees are related to your product's category.

Remember, for both selling options, there are no individual item listing fees and no credit card processing fees.

Fraud Protection

Amazon offers its sellers a world-class payment fraud protection service. They have devised a system that is ridden with personalized notifications that tell you exactly what is going on with your orders and payments at any given time.

Credit Card Facilities

Naturally, Amazon is licensed to perform secure transactions with most major credit card providers.

A-to-z Guarantee Program

This program is particularly designed for the safety of the customer but it is important to be aware of a program of this nature as it has been created to establish a sense of business confidence between the customer, Amazon and you. The A-to-z Guarantee Program has been fashioned to handle situations where a customer:

1) Never receives a product or 2) Receives a product that is different to what was ordered. The customer is initially encouraged to contact you (the seller) personally if this type of product arises. If you cannot resolve the problem, the customer can then file an 'A-to-z' claim to Amazon. Amazon then sends you an email, which outlines the customer's claim. You are requested to respond by mailing the order's basic information and an outline of the fulfillment process. Amazon will then decide how the claim will be settled - this may result in you having to refund the customer.

So now that you know how to get yourself started, you need to learn a few tricks of the trade...

It's All About The Sales, So What Can You Do To Make Sure That Your Products Sell Like Hotcakes?

Tip 1. Keywords

Appropriate keywords are vital to high product sales over the internet. Keywords drive potential customers to your product, thus it is important to try to add product specific keywords to your Amazon product description as well as anywhere else that you may be writing about your product. If you want to get really high traffic from search engines, you might need to do a keyword phrase analysis of your main product. This can be done by using Google's external keyword tool, or WordTracker's free tool. It is essential that you choose suitable keywords, with the highest rankings.

Tip 2. Write about your Products

The more online content available about your product, the better it is for sales. It is important that you write interesting content that will appeal to your market, and make sure that it contains your product's keywords.

Tip 3. Online Product Promotion Companies

Feel free to do a Google search to find a list of top product promotion companies. There are many companies available that will aggressively market your product online - with this type of external help; you won't have to personally take on the marketing of your product. The only downside about making use of these types of companies is that most of their services require you to fork out a hefty bundle of cash.

CHAPTER THREE

GARNISHING YOUR JEWELRY STORE

Simple Ways to Brighten Up Your Jewelry Store

Browsers are the bane of jewelry storeowner's lives everywhere. If every browsing customer would just buy something, you'd be swimming in cash in no time. These five things can make customers linger longer, and might just nudge them to buy something rather than go home and think about it.

    1. A small hi-fi

Size is key here, you really don't want to go overboard here with twenty speakers and bass that makes the windows rattle. Low-level backing music is relaxing on both sides of the equation - it stops you climbing the walls with boredom behind the counter, and it makes the customer feel more relaxed.

Additionally, the right music can be very effective in communicating the vibe of your brand. Are you a specialist in contemporary jewelry? Consider playing contemporary music to reinforce that brand identity.

Matching music to brand isn't essential, of course. But do consider the kinds of customers you hope to attract. People who are interested in buying modern jewelry are likely to also be interested in modern music, and hearing music that you like when you're shopping can make your stay at that store for longer than you would have otherwise - increasing the chance that they might they buy something.

2. Jewellery Display Stands

Easily overlooked. Laying jewelry out flat on low tables or shelves might seem like a good idea on paper - but determining the correct height for those tables can be difficult. You either prevent diminutive customers from seeing the whole spread of your jewelry, or you force taller customers to bend or kneel down if they want to see anything up close.

Hanging jewelry on racks isn't the best solution either. What you'll gain in terms of the sheer volume of pieces you'll be able to pile onto one rack, you'll lose invisibility. The more elaborate pieces in your inventory might need to be given their separate shelf space to allow customers to fully appreciate them.

Equally, it isn't always clear how some pieces of jewelry are supposed to be worn without using neck-shaped necklace displays, for example. Luckily manufacturers and suppliers sell displays covering jewelry of all shapes and sizes, in a range of materials.

Don't let there be any ambiguity in what the customers are seeing, they won't always ask for help if they have questions, they might just get frustrated and leave - which is the last thing you want.

3. Air Fresheners

Like the right musical backing, air fresheners, as long as they aren't too insistent, stimulate the senses of the customer through another sense entirely. Store scents can even work as fragrant business cards that they carry away in their clothes. Smelling that smell, later on, might make them recall the store, and might even make your store more central in their memory than the competition's stores.

I know that was a lot of "rights" and "cans" in quick succession, but air fresheners are such a small investment that they're worth pursuing on the off-chance that they might contribute to a customer deciding to buy something.

4. Business Cards And 5. A Physical Invoice Book

It's important to leave the customer with something to take away with them. That way, even if they decide not to buy anything, your contact information can be right in front of them in a flash. A business card in a wallet or purse, like a store's air freshener carried on clothing, can make customers remember stores that they might have forgotten about. Plus, a business card is another opportunity to communicate what makes your brand unique.

As for the physical invoice book - computers fail us as the worst possible moments. It can't hurt to have a backup plan so that a transaction can still go ahead if your computer system lets you down. You can always add the transaction to your system after the fact.

Install CCTV Cameras In Your Jewelry Stores

Although we all re□uire foolproof security and surveillance of our premises, then there is no denying to the fact that some places do require utmost levels of security and vigil. A jewelry shop is one such a place where a single mistake in security matters can create a great loss. Therefore, a jeweler must always ensure that his jewelry store has strong security system. With the advent of the digital technology, the CCTV cameras have become the most effective medium to ensure infallible security and surveillance. There are chances of committing human errors by a security person, but nothing can escape the close watch of a CCTV camera.

It is an electronic machine which capture every motion and activity, and therefore, can assist the security guards in doing their job perfectly. Nowadays, the jewelry store owners can procure the security cameras that have an inbuilt alarm facility. Installing a camera at the entrance door can provide you the full view of the person entering your store. This display on the monitor helps the security personnel to become alert and take notice any sorts of suspicious instances. The CCTV cameras have great significance, as by being alert, you can resist robbery at the very initial stage.

Proper video surveillance system can help you to from incurring big losses. In case of a loot or robbery, the footage provided by these devices can help the police authorities in catching the criminals and recovering the valuables from them. This footage also helps the store owners to review the loopholes in their surveillance systems, and fill-up all those gaps, in time. This assists them in avoiding the reoccurrence of such incidents in future. The footage provided by the CCTV cameras will also help the jewelry store owner in getting the insurance claims. The visual evidence provided by these gadgets are largely trusted and approved by most of the law enforcement authorities and insurance agencies.

Treating all the customers with dignity and respect is the only way to assure a good business relationship with them. Under the monitoring of the CCTV cameras, the customer will not feel any kind of disrespect or discomfort in the name of security and surveillance.

The installation of the CCTV cameras will also enhance the competence of the security members, by bringing to notice all the movements, within and outside the shop. These devices also make it possible for the manager to monitor all the locations at all times.

The manager can install a display unit in front of his chair and keep an eye on the customers as well as the members of the staff. All this makes the jewelry shop a secured place to deal with costly jewels and ornaments.

How to Consolidate Your Jewelry Business's Reputation

A solid reputation is worth a million bucks. Every jewelry business has a personality, and as it develops, it will become known and will make a name for itself... and it better be a good name. Here are some tips to consolidate your jewelry business's reputation:

    1. An Incredible Return Policy

Review the type of guarantee and return policy you offer your clients. It should show a high value for customer satisfaction, one the clients are surprised by, because it will give them the confidence to buy more than once, and they will feel safe. Don't be afraid to open your return policy completely. Just offer to take back any piece, at any time and for any reason, no questions asked. A 100% satisfaction guaranteed policy will show your level of trust for your product and most surely, no one will return what they bought.

    2. Valuable Incentives

Review the incentives you provide; these are a must. Customers expect them, and they put your business in the minds of your clients. They inspire loyalty and translate into more sales. An incentive is anything that gives added value to the client and pampers her while stimulating more purchases, or it can be simply a gift to someone who buys. You can put some pieces on sale, for example, the "buy 2, get 3" offer, start a 'freuent buyer' plan, or just give an unexpected gift for big orders.

3. Helping Others

It is crucial for any business, be it in wholesale jewelry or any other type, be it big or small, to have a good will principle and image. You can say it is karma. Donate a part of your sales to a good cause, donate your time, volunteer for charity events, and donate some items to worthy causes. There are many ways and opportunities to help. And, why do this? First, if you are blessed, and you most certainly are, so you should bless others. Second, it feels really good to help in some way. Thirdly, Also nice, but not as vital as the first two, it draws positive attention to your business.

CONCLUSION

Starting a jewelry business is a great way to generate some extra revenue or to start a full-time business that will help you to provide for your family. If you are someone who likes the fashion industry and the different types of jewelry that are available then you will have a lot of fun with your own jewelry business. Make sure to keep these tips in mind so that you will know which side of the business you would like to be on.

Assess your mechanical abilities and design skills. Make drawings of your ideas. First, begin designing jewelry for yourself, your family, and your friends before you actually invest much money into your business. Compare your jewelry to the competition's and research thoroughly before you try to sell yours, but don't let the competition make you fearful.

Do your research and then purchase the tools and materials that you need to make your jewelry designs. Purchase in bulk or wholesale to save on production costs. Use a spreadsheet to create an inventory system, making it easy to order supplies as you need them. Keep jewelry supply company sites as bookmarks on your computer.

List your business goals and write your business plan. Decide who your target customers will be. This will help define your choice of designs and your marketing plan. Create your niche, the designs that set your jewelry apart from the competition. Determine how much profit you want to make. Set the prices for your jewelry designs, taking into account the amount you spent for supplies, your operating costs, and your investment.

Plan where you will sell your jewelry, who is your target audience, and focus on one area or a combination of areas. Set up an online store, go to craft shows or farmer's markets, do home parties, or sell to local boutiques. Sell to your target audience on social media.

Set up your company, get a tax permit and tax identification number. Check out business insurance and get liability coverage. Get official permits and licenses. Then design a logo that can be saved on a computer and have sales flyers, cards, letterheads, and glossy brochures printed. For the financial part of your business that you don't understand, take classes and read books to learn what to do.